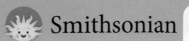 Smithsonian

DINOSAURS

Courtney Acampora

 Silver Dolphin

Silver Dolphin Books
An imprint of Printers Row Publishing Group
A division of Readerlink Distribution Services, LLC
9717 Pacific Heights Blvd, San Diego, CA 92121
www.silverdolphinbooks.com

ISBN: 978-1-64517-709-8
Manufactured, printed, and assembled in Heshan, China.
First printing, April 2021. LP/04/21
25 24 23 22 21   1 2 3 4 5

Reviewed by Matthew Miller, Museum of Natural History, Smithsonian.

For Smithsonian Enterprises:
Kealy Gordon, Product Development Manager
Jill Corcoran, Director, Licensed Publishing
Brigid Ferraro, Vice President, Consumer and Education Products
Carol LeBlanc, President

Image Credits: Thinkstock, Getty Images, Ccampodonico, Connie Ma, Dan Quinsey, James St. John: https://www.flickr.com/photos/jsjgeology/48719399856/, Jeremy Knight: https://www.flickr.com/photos/jeremyknight9/16156590681/, Luca Oddone, me_whynot, Nils Knötschke, NPS, OnFirstWhoIs, Parent Géry, Paul Hudson, The Field Museum Library: https://www.flickr.com/photos/field_museum_library/3525674419/, By The Field Museum Library - Fossil of Scelidotherium in plaster jacket, The Field Museum Library - https://www.flickr.com/photos/field_museum_library/3526481416/, USDAgov, USGS: https://library.usgs.gov/photo/#/item/51dc7dc9e4b097e4d3838db0, Yuya Tamai, Tim Evanson

CONTENTS

A NOTE TO PARENTS AND TEACHERS

All-Star Readers were created for children who are just starting on the amazing road to reading. These engaging books support the acquisition of reading skills, encourage children to learn about the world around them, and help to foster a lifelong love of books. These high-interest informational texts contain fascinating, real-world content designed to appeal to beginning readers. This early access to high-quality books provides an essential reading foundation that students will rely on throughout their school career.

The five levels in the All-Star Readers series target different stages of learning abilities. Each child is unique; age or grade level does not determine a particular reading level.

When sharing a book with beginning readers, read in short stretches, pausing often to talk about the pictures. Have younger children turn the pages and point to the pictures and familiar words. And be sure to reread favorite parts. As children become more independent readers, encourage them to share the ideas they are reading about and to discuss ideas and questions they have. Learning practice can be further extended with the quizzes after each title.

There is no right or wrong way to share books with children. You are setting a pattern of enjoying and exploring books that will set a literacy foundation for their entire school career. Find time to read with your child, and pass on the amazing world of literacy.

Adria F. Klein, Ph.D.
Professor Emeritus
California State University San Bernardino

Triassic Dinosaurs

CONTENTS

	Mesozoic	
Triassic	Jurassic	Cretaceous
252 MYA	201 MYA	145 MYA	66 MYA

Hundreds of millions of years ago, hundreds of different types of **dinosaurs** lived on Earth.

The earliest dinosaurs lived during the Triassic period.

Herrerasaurus

7

The Triassic period was from two hundred fifty-two million to two hundred one million years ago.

Earth looked very different then.

During the Triassic period, the world was warm and dry.

All of Earth's landmasses were connected.

They were connected into a supercontinent called **Pangaea**.

Triassic

NORTH AMERICA

EURASIA

PANGAEA

SOUTH AMERICA   AFRICA   Tethys Ocean

INDIA

ANTARCTICA   AUSTRALIA

Today

Arctic Ocean

NORTH AMERICA

EURASIA

Atlantic Ocean

Pacific Ocean

AFRICA

SOUTH AMERICA

Indian Ocean

Southern Ocean

ANTARCTICA

Melanorosaurus

The Triassic period followed an **extinction**.

The creatures that lived during the Triassic were survivors of the extinction.

Later, small and medium-sized dinosaurs emerged.

These were the first dinosaurs to walk the earth.

Eoraptor was an early Triassic dinosaur.

Its name means "dawn robber." It is named dawn robber because it lived at the beginning, or dawn, of the age of dinosaurs.

Eoraptor was a small and speedy dinosaur. Its **fossil** was first discovered in Argentina in 1991.

Eoraptor ran quickly on its hind legs.

Its long, flexible neck helped it look around for **prey**.

Scientists believe that *Eoraptor* ate both plants and meat.

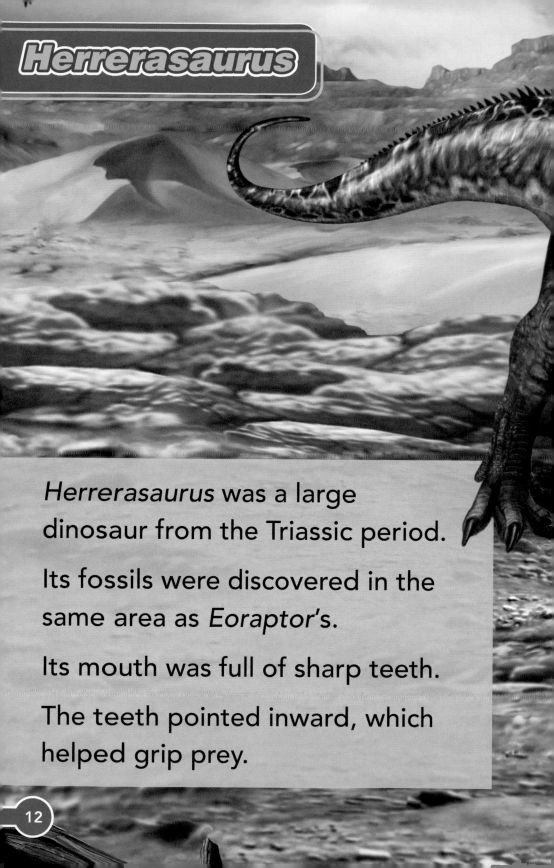

Herrerasaurus

Herrerasaurus was a large dinosaur from the Triassic period.

Its fossils were discovered in the same area as *Eoraptor*'s.

Its mouth was full of sharp teeth.

The teeth pointed inward, which helped grip prey.

This meat eater was about the size of a horse.

It is estimated that *Herrerasaurus*'s strong back legs allowed it to run twenty-three miles per hour.

That's faster than an Olympic runner!

Coelophysis was a **carnivore**.

This meat eater's narrow jaw was full of razor-sharp teeth.

Coelophysis weighed up to forty-four pounds.

Coelophysis, like many meat-eating dinosaurs, had a wishbone like modern-day birds!

Coelophysis belonged to a group of dinosaurs called **theropods**.

Coelophysis often traveled in groups, which gave them extra protection while hunting for larger animals.

Plateosaurus

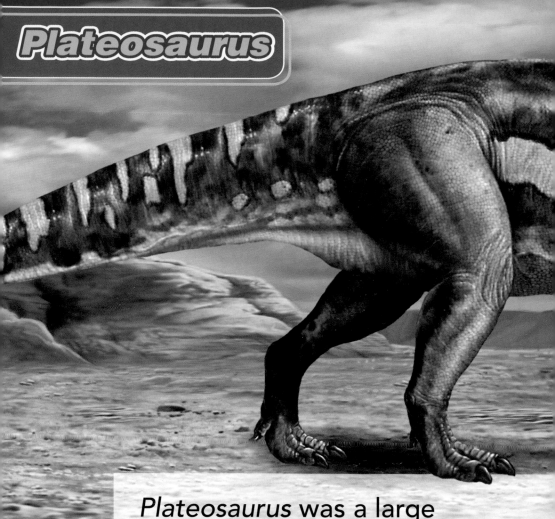

Plateosaurus was a large dinosaur called a **prosauropod**.

It was an ancestor to the large **sauropods** that lived millions of years later.

The first *Plateosaurus* fossils were found in Germany in 1834.

Plateosaurus was a plant eater.

This **herbivore** had a long neck and strong hind legs.

It reared up on its legs to reach leaves high in the treetops.

It is one of the most scientifically well-known Triassic dinosaurs.

Saltopus

Saltopus was a small meat eater that was about the size of a cat.

Its name means "leaping foot." *Saltopus* fossils were discovered in a **quarry** in Scotland.

Saltopus's sharp eyesight helped it hunt at night.

It was able to catch prey that other predators were unable to see at night.

Saltopus's long legs helped it move quickly across its habitat.

Chindesaurus

Chindesaurus was one of the first dinosaurs in North America.

Its fossils were discovered in Petrified Forest National Park in Arizona.

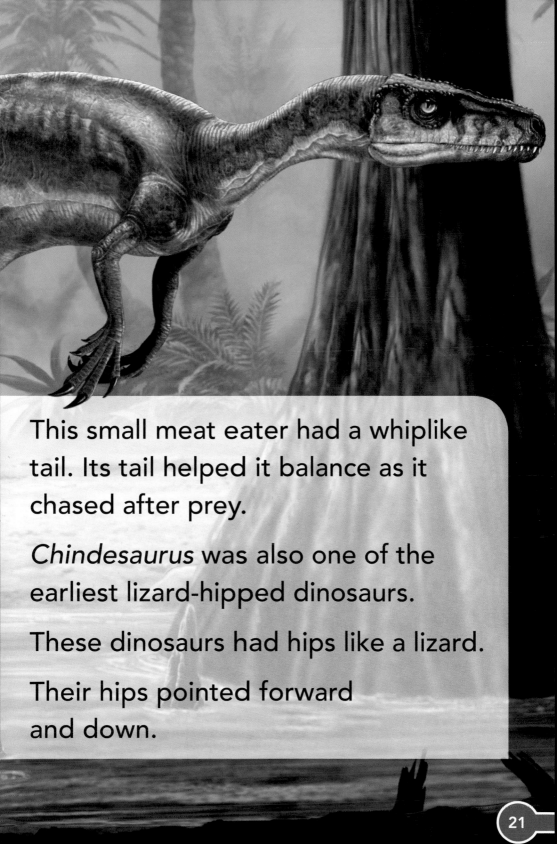

This small meat eater had a whiplike tail. Its tail helped it balance as it chased after prey.

Chindesaurus was also one of the earliest lizard-hipped dinosaurs.

These dinosaurs had hips like a lizard.

Their hips pointed forward and down.

Riojasaurus

Riojasaurus was a plant eater that used its long neck to search for leaves in the trees.

It had a large, bulky body. It was unable to walk on its hands so it got around on its hind legs.

Riojasaurus was one of the earliest giant plant eaters.

At thirty-six feet long, this large dinosaur's bones had air sacs in them.

The air sacs made its bones lighter so this bulky dinosaur could move around easily.

Melanorosaurus was a large plant-eating dinosaur.

It was one of the earliest long-necked plant eaters.

Because of its large size, it walked around on four thick legs instead of two legs.

Melanorosaurus means "Black Mountain lizard."

Its fossils were discovered on Black Mountain in Transkei, South Africa.

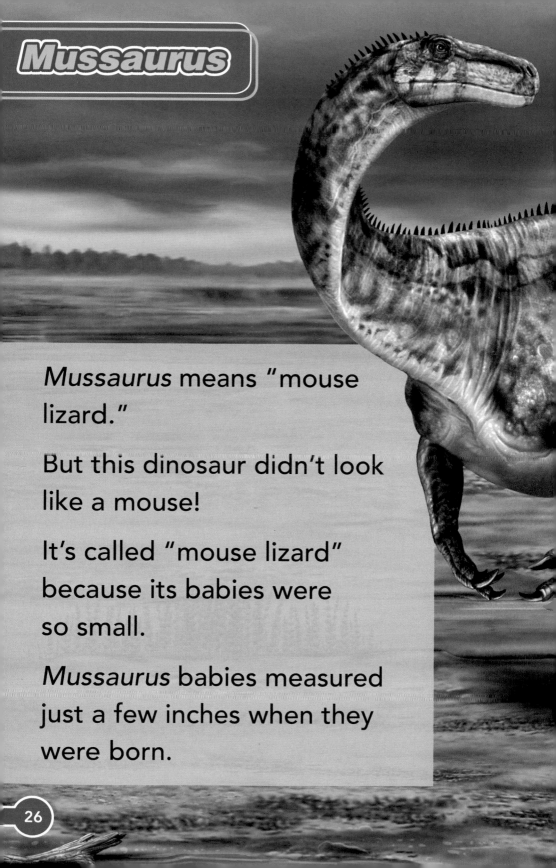

Mussaurus means "mouse lizard."

But this dinosaur didn't look like a mouse!

It's called "mouse lizard" because its babies were so small.

Mussaurus babies measured just a few inches when they were born.

Mussaurus babies first got around by crawling on all fours, similar to human babies.

Then, like humans, the *Mussaurus* babies would learn to walk on two legs.

Staurikosaurus

Staurikosaurus was a small meat eater that fed on small reptiles or dinosaur babies.

Its fossils were discovered in Brazil in South America.

Staurikosaurus's hind legs were long, which helped it move quickly.

Its sharp teeth pointed inward.

When *Staurikosaurus* caught its prey, its teeth made sure the prey wouldn't slip out of its mouth.

Guaibasaurus

Guaibasaurus was a meat eater.

This dinosaur ran on two legs and used the sharp claws on its hands to grip prey.

The fossil of this small dinosaur was first discovered in Brazil in South America.

Guaibasaurus is a dinosaur that has puzzled scientists.

They discovered that *Guaibasaurus* was an ancestor to both theropods and sauropods.

This is important because it helps scientists understand how both theropods and sauropods **evolved**.

Terrific Triassic Dinosaurs

Earth's earliest dinosaurs are some of the most mysterious.

Though scientists believed that Triassic dinosaurs were all small, new discoveries have proven otherwise.

Scientists have used their findings to figure out how dinosaurs evolved and what life was like during the Triassic period.

With each new discovery, scientists learn more about the fierce meat eaters and giant plant eaters that lived millions of years after the Triassic.

1. What was Pangaea?
   a) A plant that grew in South America
   b) A very small dinosaur
   c) A supercontinent made up of all the landmasses on Earth

2. What was the earth like during the Triassic period?
   a) It was frozen
   b) It was warm and dry
   c) It was half swamp and half frozen

3. What happened before the Triassic period?
   a) Earth was covered in ice
   b) There was an extinction
   c) The biggest dinosaurs lived

4. What helped plant eaters reach leaves in the treetops?
   a) Long hands
   b) Wings
   c) Long necks

5. What did *Riojasaurus*'s bones have in them?
   a) Air sacs
   b) Eggs
   c) Pigments

6. Which dinosaur first crawled on all fours and then walked on two legs as it grew up?
   a) *Mussaurus*
   b) *Plateosaurus*
   c) *Herrerasaurus*

Glossary

carnivore an animal that eats meat

dinosaurs prehistoric reptiles that lived on land more than 66 million years ago

evolved when an animal group changed over time to better help them survive

extinction a process in which a group of related animals are no longer living

fossil remains of an animal or plant that have been turned to stone over a long period of time

herbivore an animal that eats only plants

Pangaea a supercontinent made up of all the landmasses on Earth

prey an animal that is hunted by other animals for food

prosauropod a large dinosaur from the Triassic and Jurassic periods that had a long neck and tail, a small head, and ate plants

quarry a pit dug by people looking for stone or other materials, including fossils

sauropods large dinosaurs that ate plants; most sauropods had a long neck, long tail, and a small head

theropods dinosaurs that usually ate meat and walked on two legs; most theropods had small forelimbs

Jurassic Dinosaurs

CONTENTS

Mesozoic		
Triassic	Jurassic	Cretaceous
252 MYA	201 MYA	145 MYA	66 MYA

After the Triassic period was the Jurassic period.

The Jurassic period was from two hundred one million to one hundred forty-five million years ago.

During the Jurassic period, Earth was generally warmer and wetter than it is today.

Diplodocus

39

The Jurassic Period

During the Jurassic period, the land was covered in trees, ferns, and other plants.

Some of the biggest and most recognizable dinosaurs lived during the Jurassic period.

Ceratosaurus

Two hundred million years ago, Pangaea began breaking up; a process that would take millions of years.

Two big **continents** were created.

They were called Laurasia and Gondwana.

Laurasia was in the northern **hemisphere**. Gondwana was in the southern hemisphere.

Brachiosaurus

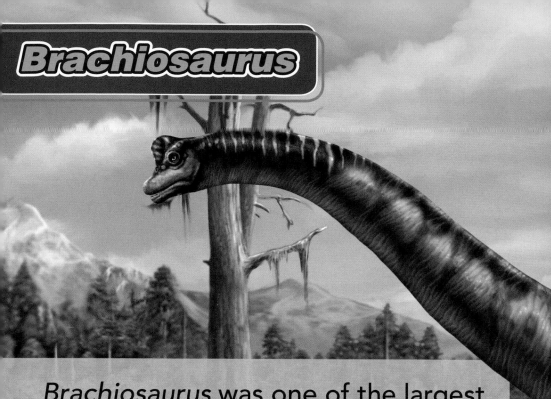

Brachiosaurus was one of the largest animals to ever walk the earth.

Brachiosaurus was an **herbivore**.

It ate four hundred pounds of plants a day!

Brachiosaurus means "arm lizard."

Brachiosaurus earned its name because its front legs were longer than its back legs.

Brachiosaurus's long neck helped it reach leaves that other dinosaurs couldn't reach.

Its neck measured forty feet long.

Brachiosaurus weighed as much as twelve African elephants.

Diplodocus

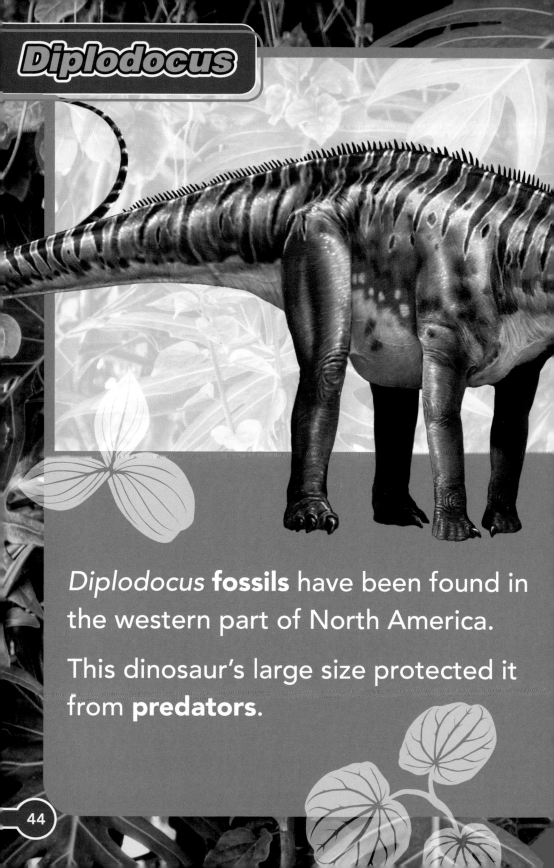

Diplodocus **fossils** have been found in the western part of North America.

This dinosaur's large size protected it from **predators**.

Diplodocus had peglike teeth that it used to comb leaves off branches like a rake.

It likely swallowed its food whole.

Diplodocus also ate stones to help it digest its food.

Today, some birds swallow stones for this reason too.

Apatosaurus

At sixty-nine feet long, *Apatosaurus* was a true giant.

Apatosaurus laid some of the largest eggs of any dinosaur.

Each egg was about the size of a basketball!

Apatosaurus mothers laid their eggs in clusters of up to ten.

Camptosaurus was a bird-hipped dinosaur that lived in present-day Wyoming.

Its hips pointed backward like a bird's.

This plant eater lived in groups.

It used its speed to escape from predators.

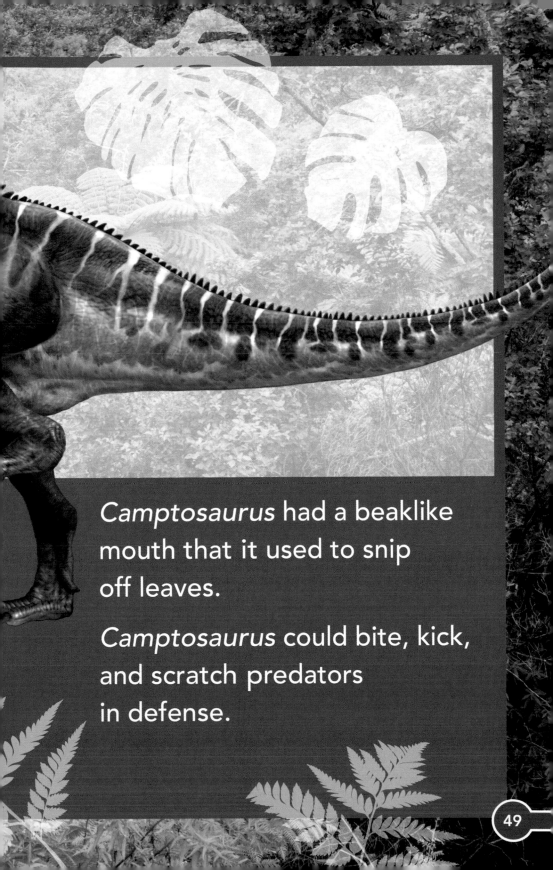

Camptosaurus had a beaklike mouth that it used to snip off leaves.

Camptosaurus could bite, kick, and scratch predators in defense.

Stegosaurus

Stegosaurus was a plant eater.

This dinosaur's front legs were shorter than its back legs.

This made *Stegosaurus*'s head low to the ground.

It was easier for *Stegosaurus* to eat short plants.

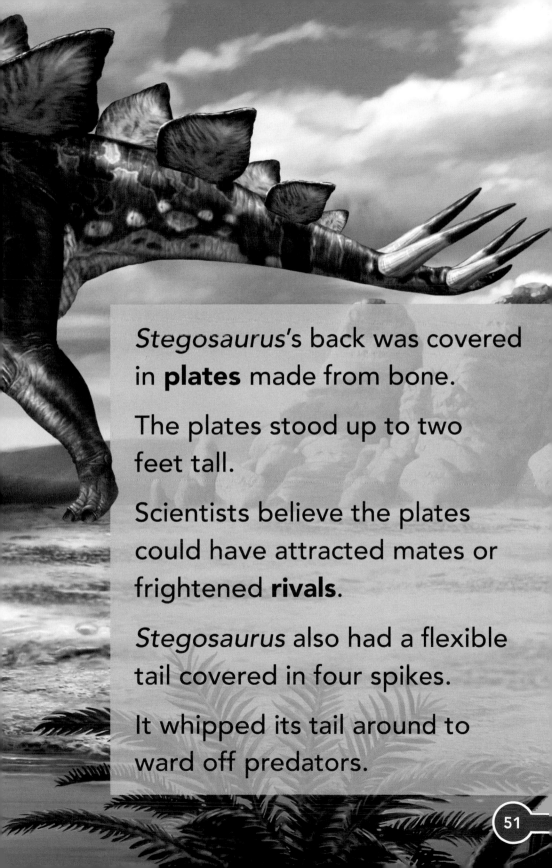

Stegosaurus's back was covered in **plates** made from bone.

The plates stood up to two feet tall.

Scientists believe the plates could have attracted mates or frightened **rivals**.

Stegosaurus also had a flexible tail covered in four spikes.

It whipped its tail around to ward off predators.

Allosaurus

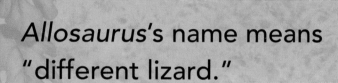

Allosaurus's name means "different lizard."

It got its name because its neck bones looked different than the neck bones of other dinosaurs.

Allosaurus was half the size of *T. rex*, but it was still a fierce predator.

Scientists have discovered tooth marks on *Allosaurus* fossils.

This suggests that they may have eaten each other!

Their backward-facing teeth made sure prey stayed inside their mouth.

Allosaurus could also open its jaw extremely wide to gobble up its prey.

Anchiornis

Anchiornis was a **unique** dinosaur because it had four wings but did not fly.

Anchiornis had curved claws to catch prey.

This dinosaur's fossil was discovered in China in 2009.

Scientists discovered **melanosomes** in the fossil.

Melanosomes produce color in animals' feathers, hair, skin, and eyes.

Scientists learned that *Anchiornis* had black and white feathers and a red **crest** on its head.

The crest may have been used to attract mates.

Camarasaurus

Camarasaurus was a fifty-foot-long plant eater that lived in present-day North America.

This sauropod's fossils are commonly found in the Morrison Formation.

The Morrison Formation is a fossil-rich rock layer in the western United States.

Camarasaurus means "chambered lizard" because there were air sac chambers in its **vertebrae**.

The air sacs made the bones lighter.

This reduced the dinosaur's hefty weight.

Ceratosaurus

Ceratosaurus means "horned lizard."

This carnivore had a horn on its nose and horns above its eyes.

Ceratosaurus was the second-largest predator of its time.

The largest was *Allosaurus*.

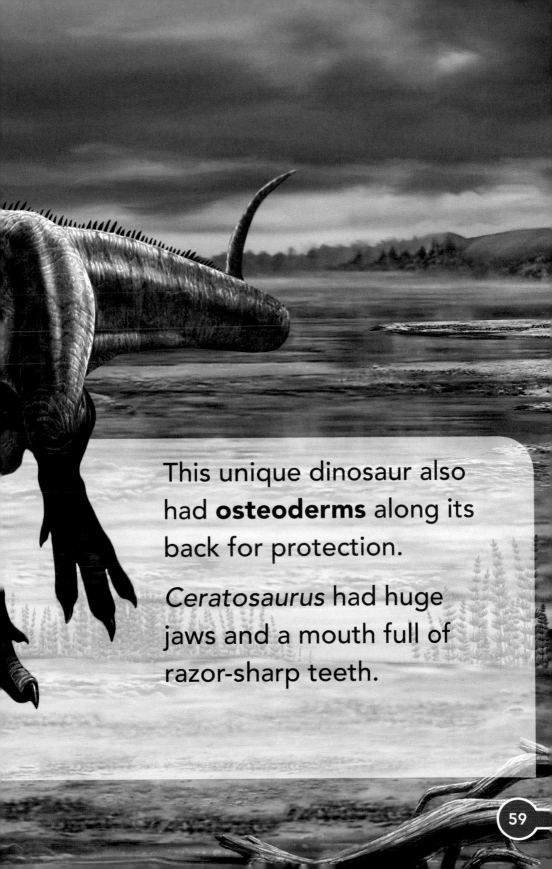

This unique dinosaur also had **osteoderms** along its back for protection.

Ceratosaurus had huge jaws and a mouth full of razor-sharp teeth.

Kentrosaurus was a small cousin of *Stegosaurus*.

A *Kentrosaurus* fossil was first discovered in Tanzania in Africa.

At one site, nine hundred *Kentrosaurus* bones were found!

This dinosaur's name means "sharp-pointed lizard" because it shoulders, back, and tail were covered in spikes.

Kentrosaurus had a flexible tail.

The spiky tail was used to fend off predators.

Mamenchisaurus

Mamenchisaurus was a plant-eating sauropod.

Mamenchisaurus had the longest neck of any dinosaur compared to its total body length.

Mamenchisaurus's neck was half its total body length.

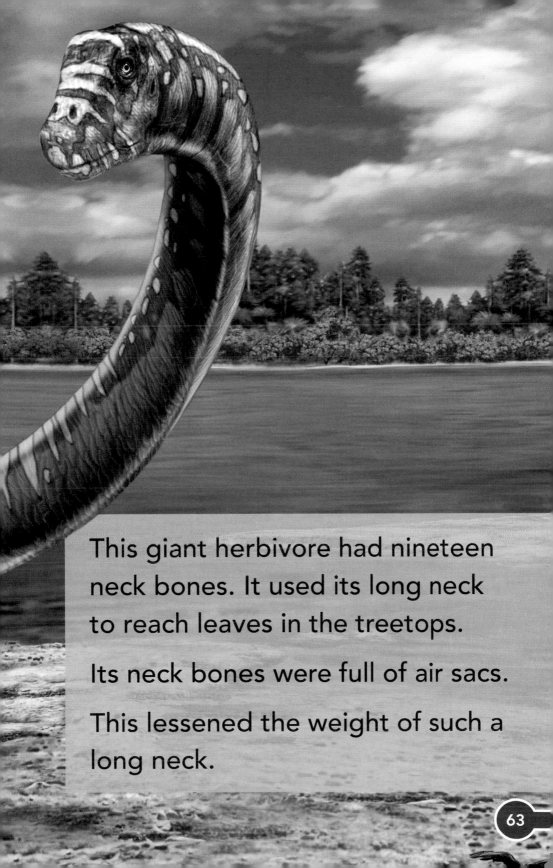

This giant herbivore had nineteen neck bones. It used its long neck to reach leaves in the treetops.

Its neck bones were full of air sacs.

This lessened the weight of such a long neck.

Walking with the Jurassic Dinosaurs

As the earth continued changing and continents broke apart, some dinosaurs evolved into larger creatures.

Many of the largest dinosaurs lived during the Jurassic period.

These dinosaurs ruled the earth and set the stage for the fierce dinosaurs that were to come.

1. What was the
   Jurassic Period
   like on Earth?
   a) Warm and wet
   b) Frozen
   c) Hot and dry

2. How big were *Apatosaurus*'s eggs?
   a) The size of a golf ball
   b) The size of a boulder
   c) The size of a basketball

3. What do melanosomes reveal?
   a) How many teeth a dinosaur had
   b) The color of a dinosaur
   c) How long a dinosaur's tail was

4. Why did some dinosaurs have air sacs in their bones?
   a) Because these dinosaurs were smaller in size
   b) To lessen the weight of the bones
   c) To float in the water

5. What were osteoderms used for?
   a) Protecting the body
   b) Digesting food
   c) Eyesight

6. Which dinosaur had the longest neck for its body size?
   a) *Apatosaurus*
   b) *Mamenchisaurus*
   c) *Ceratosaurus*

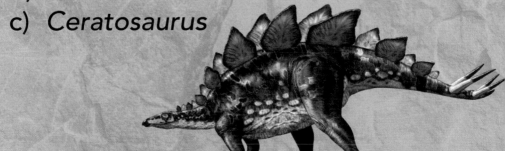

Glossary

continents the main large landmasses on Earth

crest skin, fur, or feathers that grow upward on an animal's head; crests sometimes continue down an animal's back

fossils remains of animals or plants that have been turned to stone over a long period of time

hemisphere a half of the earth split by the equator, an imaginary line that runs around the center of the earth

herbivore an animal that eats only plants

melanosomes parts of cells where skin or hair color is created and stored

osteoderms bones embedded in the skin of animals that help them protect themselves

plates flat parts of an animal's body that form a structure

predators animals that hunt and eat other animals for food

rivals animal competitors that want the same food or mates

unique unlike anything else

vertebrae bones that make up the spine

Cretaceous Dinosaurs

CONTENTS

The Cretaceous Period

After the Jurassic period, dinosaurs continued to thrive.

The Cretaceous period was from one hundred forty-five million to sixty-six million years ago.

New dinosaurs evolved and became more **diverse**.

But at the end of the Cretaceous period, all of the dinosaurs, except for birds, went **extinct**.

During the Cretaceous period, the continents continued to break apart.

They moved toward the positions that they occupy today.

There were no polar ice caps at this time because Earth was so warm.

Corythosaurus

Paleontologists have found **fossils** of the first true birds and flowering plants from the Cretaceous period.

By this period, dinosaurs had been around so long that fossils of earlier dinosaurs were buried beneath their feet!

Tyrannosaurus rex (T. rex)

Tyrannosaurus rex was a fierce hunter with lots of sharp teeth and a powerful bite.

Its arms were small and short, but surprisingly strong.

Like today's birds, *Tyrannosaurus* rex walked on its toes.

Tyrannosaurus rex's mouth was filled with twelve-inch-long teeth.

Its teeth were ridged and made to tear through meat.

It could eat one hundred pounds of meat in one bite!

Triceratops

Triceratops means "three-horned face."

Triceratops earned this name because it had three sharp horns on its head.

It also had a big **frill** on its neck.

Triceratops had a sharp beak used to crush through tough plants.

Its teeth were continuously shed and replaced throughout its life.

It had short, strong legs with hooflike toes.

Ankylosaurus

Ankylosaurus was the size of a small truck.

Its name means "fused lizard" because it was covered in fused, armored plates.

The bony plates protected it from predators, such as *T. rex*.

Ankylosaurus's tail had a bony knob that it swung like a club.

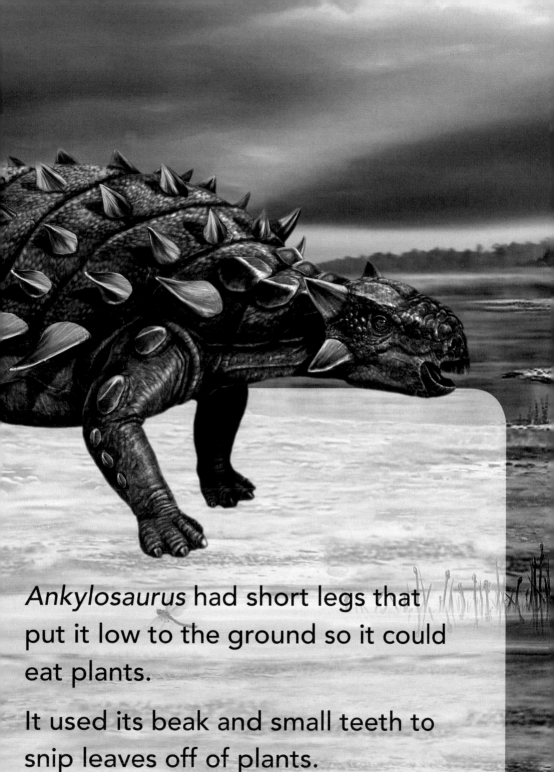

Ankylosaurus had short legs that put it low to the ground so it could eat plants.

It used its beak and small teeth to snip leaves off of plants.

Iguanodon

An *Iguanodon* fossil was one of the first fossils to be recognized as a dinosaur.

Iguanodon was a plant eater that was twice the weight of an elephant.

Iguanodon means "iguana tooth." Its teeth looked like those of modern iguanas.

Iguanodon walked on four legs but could run on two legs for short distances.

It had padded, webbed hands.

Iguanodon also had sharp spikes on its thumbs.

Majungasaurus

In 1895, French soldiers found fossils in Madagascar, an island off the coast of Africa.

These fossils belonged to a dinosaur called *Majungasaurus*.

This carnivore was a fierce hunter that is known to have eaten members of its own **species**.

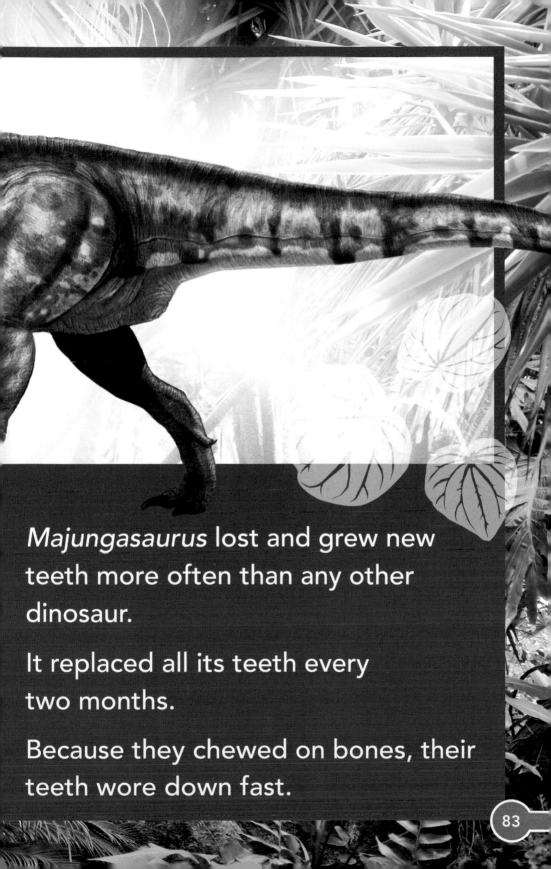

Majungasaurus lost and grew new teeth more often than any other dinosaur.

It replaced all its teeth every two months.

Because they chewed on bones, their teeth wore down fast.

Velociraptor

Velociraptor was a fierce, speedy dinosaur. Its name means "fast thief."

It was an aggressive hunter, but was only the size of a large turkey.

Velociraptor moved around on two legs and could run quickly.

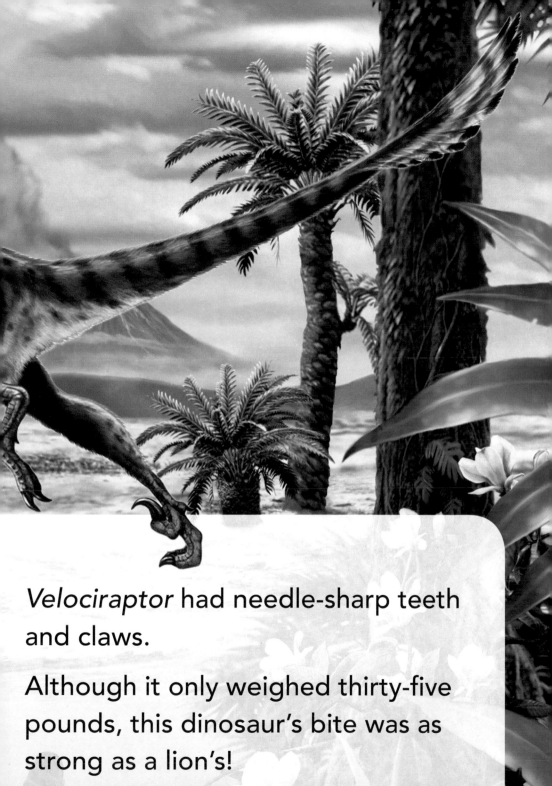

Velociraptor had needle-sharp teeth and claws.

Although it only weighed thirty-five pounds, this dinosaur's bite was as strong as a lion's!

Maiasaura

Maiasaura was a duck-billed dinosaur called a **hadrosaur.**

Seventy-five million years ago, a **herd** of *Maiasaura* was killed and covered by volcanic ash.

Scientists learned about old and young dinosaurs by studying the fossilized remains of the herd and their eggs.

Maiasaura mothers nested together in groups.

Scientists learned that *Maiasaura* took good care of its young.

Maiasaura means "good mother lizard."

Giganotosaurus

Giganotosaurus was one of the largest meat-eating dinosaurs.

It was even larger than *Tyrannosaurus rex!*

Giganotosaurus lived thirty million years before *Tyrannosaurus rex.*

Giganotosaurus roamed the swamplands searching for prey.

It could run up to twenty miles per hour and slice into its prey with razor-sharp teeth.

Avimimus

Avimimus was a small meat-eating dinosaur.

It had a long neck and legs and looked a bit like a small ostrich.

It was covered in feathers, but could not fly.

Avimimus had short arms that were able to fold up like a modern bird's.

Each arm had three sharp claws on the ends.

Pachycephalosaurus

Pachycephalosaurus's name means "thick-headed lizard" because its skull could be up to nine inches thick.

Its skull was hard and not easily damaged.

Skulls are often the only Pachycephalosaurus remains found by scientists today.

Pachycephalosaurus heads had a circle of spikes on top.

Some scientists believe that *Pachycephalosauruses* butted heads like bighorn sheep.

Spinosaurus was a carnivore that walked around on two legs. It was larger than *T. rex.*

It had a large **sail** on its back that stood up to six feet tall.

Spinosaurus had a long, thin snout that helped it catch fish.

Its teeth pointed inward, which helped fish stay in its mouth as it scooped them up.

The End of the Dinosaurs

Dinosaurs ruled Earth for one hundred sixty-five million years. At the end of the Cretaceous period, they became extinct.

Scientists discovered an **asteroid** had smashed into Earth.

This cooled the planet, killing a wide variety of plant and animal life.

Millions of years later, humans discovered dinosaur fossils.

These fossils revealed the magnificent world of the dinosaurs.

There is still so much more to discover!

1. What were dinosaurs' ridged teeth used for?
   a) To sharpen their claws
   b) To tear through meat
   c) To make a loud whistle call

2. What does "*Triceratops*" mean?
   a) Three-horned face
   b) Swift runner
   c) Fancy frill

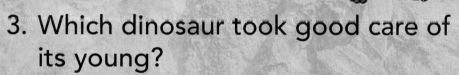

3. Which dinosaur took good care of its young?
   a) *Tyrannosaurus rex*
   b) *Maiasaura*
   c) *Ankylosaurus*

4. Which meat eater was larger than *Tyrannosaurus rex*?
   a) *Giganotosaurus*
   b) *Velociraptor*
   c) *Avimimus*

5. Why did *Pachycephalosaurus* have a thick skull?
   a) To hold its large brain
   b) To butt heads with other *Pachycephalosauruses*
   c) To control its body temperature

6. Which of the below is true about *Spinosaurus*?
   a) It had webbed feet for paddling
   b) It had a thin snout for catching fish
   c) It could hold its breath for five minutes

Glossary

asteroid a small rocky body that orbits the sun

diverse having different qualities or characteristics

extinct no longer living

fossils remains of animals or plants that have been turned to stone over a long period of time

frill a fringe of feathers or bony body part that sticks up around an animal's neck

hadrosaur a type of plant-eating dinosaur with a duck-billed mouth

herd a group of animals

paleontologists scientists who study fossils

sail the large, sometimes spiky part of a dinosaur that sticks out of its back

species a group of living things different from all other groups

Digging for Dinosaurs

CONTENTS

All About Paleontologists

Paleontologists study **fossils** to understand what life was like long ago.

But you don't have to be a paleontologist to study fossils.

Everyday people, even kids, find fossils too!

Only about one out of one hundred fossils is actually discovered by a scientist.

Paleontologists at Work

Many paleontologists love **fieldwork**! It's exciting to discover something no one has seen before.

After a paleontologist finds a fossil, it is carefully sent back to a lab to be studied closely.

Paleontologists study fossils to learn about new dinosaurs.

Sometimes they learn more about **species** that have been known about for some time.

They also learn more about Earth's natural history.

Some fossils are cleaned and displayed in museums.

Everything we know about dinosaurs comes from their fossils and today's birds.

Fossils are the remains of animals preserved in the earth.

Birds are dinosaurs' **descendants**.

Dinosaur fossils formed because the dinosaurs' bodies were covered by mud or sand in a wet environment.

After a long time, minerals in the sediment replaced parts of the bone.

Fossils are rock and are exact copies of the original bones.

Paleontologists find fossils of everything from bones and teeth to footprints.

Fossils of teeth determine if a dinosaur was a plant eater or a meat eater.

Fossilized footprints show how dinosaurs moved and whether they traveled in herds.

What fossils can reveal:	What fossils can't reveal:
• A dinosaur's size • Its body shape • How it moved	• The sounds it made • Body parts that don't fossilize

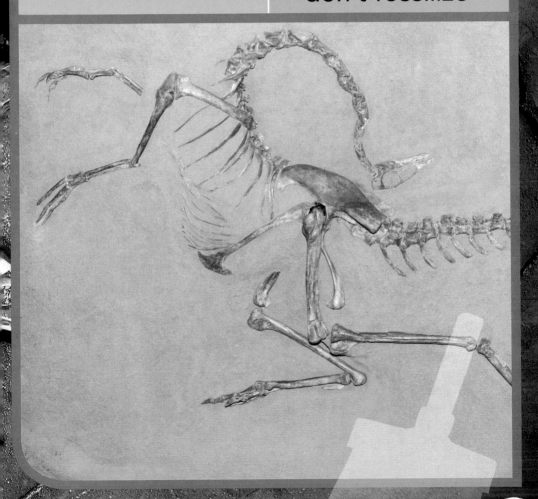

Dinosaur Bones

Dinosaur skeletons on display at museums look complete, but that's not how they are usually discovered.

Big bones are easier to find.

Tiny bones can be taken away by predators, moved by wind, or washed away by rain.

Paleontologists often find more of one type of bone because the dinosaur had more of them.

For example, ribs and vertebrae are easier to find than a skull.

Paleontologists put all the bones together like a puzzle.

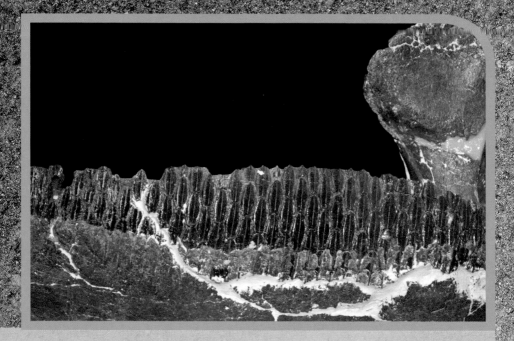

Dinosaur teeth reveal what a dinosaur's diet was like.

Meat eaters had long, **serrated** teeth like a steak knife.

Plant eaters had peglike teeth for crushing plants or raking leaves off branches.

Dinosaurs continually lost and replaced their teeth throughout their lives.

Diplodocus, a plant eater, may have replaced one tooth a month!

Lost teeth are very common fossils for scientists to find.

Amazing Amber

Amber is fossilized tree **resin**.

As it hardens, insects and other creatures can get trapped inside.

Sometimes, the animal was alive when it got trapped in amber.

The amber preserves the creature in its complete form.

Amber is usually yellow, but it can also be brown, red, orange, and blue.

In 2016, researchers in China found part of a dinosaur tail preserved in amber.

The tail feathers were even intact!

Fieldwork is work done in nature instead of in a lab.

Scientists often know of an area where finding fossils is likely.

Once a fossil is found, it's time to **excavate**!

In the field, a lot of work is done by hand, but tools make it easier.

Paleontologists use hammers, chisels, small picks, and brushes.

When a fossil is found, it is important to find its edges and expose its top to make sure it's complete enough to remove.

A trench is dug around it so the fossil can eventually be removed.

The fossil is removed in a big chunk and covered in a **field jacket**.

It is important to keep the fossil safe and in one piece.

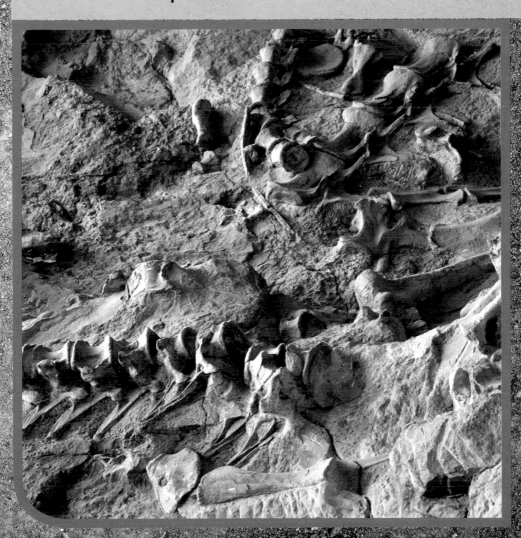

Moving and Recording Fossils

When a fossil is unearthed, it is very **fragile**.

Field jackets protect fossils from weather or accidental damage and help keep together the rock the fossil is in.

The field jackets must be strong enough to protect the fossil as it is transported to a lab or museum.

But they must also be able to be taken apart easily without damaging the fossil so scientists can study the fossil in the lab.

How Field Jackets Are Made

First, scientists apply wet toilet paper to the fossil.

Then burlap strips covered in **plaster** are put on top.

The plaster is smoothed out and dries into a protective shell so the fossil can be moved to a lab.

At the lab, the field jacket is removed and the fossil is cleaned off so scientists can study it.

Paleontologists measure, draw, and describe the fossil.

They compare the fossil to other dinosaur fossils.

If it's a fossil from a new dinosaur, they'll name the dinosaur.

Paleontology Today and Tomorrow

Technology helps scientists and paleontologists.

3D modeling and printing allows scientists to create an image of what the dinosaur looked like.

X-rays allow scientists to look at fossils closer than ever before.

Sometimes, paleontologists learn something new about dinosaurs that were discovered years earlier.

Because new fossils are still being found, what we know about dinosaurs is constantly changing.

Scientists now know that modern birds are the last living relatives of the dinosaurs.

They are ancestors of dinosaurs called **theropods**.

We know that *T. rex*, one of the biggest and scariest dinosaurs, is more closely related to birds than it is to any other animal living today!

Next time you see a bird in the sky, think about how it came from ancestors that ruled the prehistoric world.

1. What can a fossil NOT reveal?
   a) A dinosaur's body shape
   b) The sounds a dinosaur made
   c) How a dinosaur moved

2. Which types of bones do paleontologists often find more of?
   a) Vertebrae
   b) Skulls
   c) Hip bones

3. Which is NOT a type of fossil?
   a) Muscle
   b) Dung
   c) Bone

4. What is amber?
   a) Fossilized tree resin
   b) A type of coral
   c) Fossilized quartz

5. What is coprolite?
   a) Jacket plaster
   b) Fossilized feather
   c) Fossilized dung

6. Why do scientists put jackets on fossils?
   a) To display them in museums
   b) To protect them from weather or damage
   c) To prepare them for photos

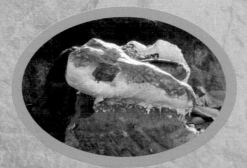

Glossary

coprolite fossilized dinosaur dung

descendants animals that are distantly related to an animal that lived long ago

excavate removing something from the ground by digging

field jacket a plaster covering around a fossil to protect it while being transported to a lab

fieldwork scientific research that happens in the natural environment

fossils remains of animals or plants that have been turned to stone over a long period of time

fragile easily broken or harmed

paleontologists scientists who study fossils

plaster a pasty mixture of lime, sand, or cement and water that hardens when it dries

resin a sticky substance from trees and other plants

serrated having jagged or sawlike edges

species a group of living things different from all other groups

theropods dinosaurs that usually ate meat and walked on two legs; most theropods had small forelimbs